I Can Volunteer

By Maria Nelson

Gareth Stevens
Publishing

Please visit our website, www.garethstevens.com. For a free color catalog of all our high-quality books, call toll free 1-800-542-2595 or fax 1-877-542-2596.

Nelson, Maria.
I can volunteer / by Maria Nelson.
   p. cm. — (Kids of character)
Includes index.
ISBN 978-1-4339-9038-0 (pbk.)
ISBN 978-1-4339-9039-7 (6-pack)
ISBN 978-1-4339-9037-3 (library binding)
1. Voluntarism—Juvenile literature. 2. Young volunteers—Juvenile literature. I. Nelson, Maria. II. Title.
HN49.V64 N45 2014
361.37—dc23

First Edition

Published in 2014 by
Gareth Stevens Publishing
111 East 14th Street, Suite 349
New York, NY 10003

Designer: Nicholas Domiano
Editor: Kristen Rajczak

Photo credits: Cover, p. 1 © iStockphoto.com/asiseeit; pp. 5, 9 Creatas/Thinkstock.com; p. 7 Photos.com/Thinkstock.com; pp. 11, 17 iStockphoto/Thinkstock.com; p. 13 Lisa F. Young/Shutterstock.com; p. 15 SelectStock/the Agency Collection/Getty Images; p. 19 Comstock/Thinkstock.com; p. 21 KidStock/Blend Images/Getty Images.

Printed in the United States of America

CPSIA compliance information: Batch #CS13GS: For further information contact Gareth Stevens, New York, New York at 1-800-542-2595.

Contents

What Is Volunteering? 4

Neighborhood Helpers 6

School Volunteers. 10

Communities in Need 14

Glossary. 22

For More Information. 23

Index .24

Boldface words appear in the glossary.

What Is Volunteering?

A volunteer is a person who works without pay. Volunteering often means helping those in need. Sometimes people who want to volunteer join a group. Others start a group or volunteer on their own!

Neighborhood Helpers

Dimitri's neighborhood had many older people living in it. When it snowed, he volunteered to shovel their driveways. He also spread special salt to melt the ice on the sidewalks. Dimitri helped those who needed it.

Paolo thought the park near his house was a mess! He asked his friends and neighbors to help him clean it up. The volunteers worked together to pick up trash, plant new trees, and put in new swings!

School Volunteers

Alaina's little sister worried about missing her bus after school. Other kids worried, too. Alaina and a teacher **organized** a group of older students to walk younger students to their buses so they got there on time each day.

Rebecca was great at math! Her teacher asked her to volunteer as a **tutor**. She helped other students with their math homework after school. Like Rebecca, volunteers often use their strengths to help others.

Communities in Need

The community center near Jaime's house was collecting clothes for those in need. Her mom helped her gather a big box of clothes to give. They also joined a group of volunteers who sorted the clothes.

Dorothy was so excited to volunteer at the animal **shelter**. She loved to feed the kittens and walk the dogs. Dorothy even got to brush the horses! It's fun to volunteer doing something you enjoy.

Ed and his school chorus volunteered to sing at his grandma's **nursing home**. They picked songs everyone would know. His grandma and her friends enjoyed the singing. Ed visited with them after he sang, too.

Trinity learned about her town's past while doing a school project. After it was done, she still wanted to know more! Trinity asked the history **museum** if she could help there. Many community organizations look for interested volunteers!

Glossary

museum: a building in which things of interest are displayed

nursing home: a place where those who are old or sick and need help live

organize: to put together in an orderly way

shelter: a place where animals or people are kept safe

tutor: a person who helps someone with schoolwork

For More Information

Books

Antill, Sara. *10 Ways I Can Help My Community*. New York, NY: PowerKids Press, 2012.

Borus, Audrey. *Volunteering: A How-To Guide*. Berkeley Heights, NJ: Enslow Publishers, 2011.

Websites

Be a Volunteer

kidshealth.org/kid/feeling/thought/volunteering.html

Read more about volunteering, including how to get started.

GenerationOn

www.generationon.org/kids

Learn why you should volunteer, and find lots of ideas about how you can help your community.

Index

animal shelter 16

clean up 8

clothes 14

community
    organizations
    20

group 4, 10, 14

helping 4, 6, 8, 12,
    14, 20

museum 20

need 4, 6, 14

nursing home 18

organize 10

shovel driveways 6

tutor 12